C

Teachers' notes

Aims of this book

▲ To develop ideas about the life processes common to animals and those common to plants;
▲ To introduce ideas about caring for animals and plants;
▲ To learn about the structure of plants and the life-cycle of flowering plants;
▲ To provide practice in sorting and classifying animals and plants;
▲ To learn about the habitats of animals and plants and the interrelationships between them;
▲ To provide experience in observing, predicting, measuring, recording and drawing conclusions.

Developing science skills

While it is not necessary to work through the activity sheets in order, all those covering one subject should be dealt with at the same time.

Although it is in 'doing' science that children learn best, they also need to observe, record, predict, measure, look for patterns, classify, explain and ask questions leading to further investigation. They need to discuss their work, before and after the activity.

Safety precautions

Visit a site for field work beforehand to assess any safety concerns. Ensure there are enough adult helpers and that the children are suitably dressed. Close supervision is essential where water is involved.

Establish a code of conduct before the visit. This could include walking quietly, replacing things as they were found, not dropping litter, closing farm gates and taking care of plants and animals found. Show them how to gather small animals carefully using a plastic spoon and a paintbrush. All creatures should be returned to their natural habitat. Allow the children to become familiar with equipment to be used before the visit.

Scientific background

This information aims to help you to understand the scientific concepts and ideas covered in this book. It generally goes beyond the level of understanding expected of most children, but will give you the confidence to ask and answer questions and to guide the children in their investigations.

Animals have particular life processes such as feeding, breathing, growth and reproduction which are common to all animals, including humans.

All animals can move in some way, but some are able to move more freely than others. Sessile animals (such as the sea anemone) are fixed in one place but they can move their body parts to obtain food or retract from enemies. Freedom of movement is essential for an animal's chances of survival as it enables it to hunt for food, find suitable places to live, find a mate and escape from predators.

All animals have to eat. The consumed food is converted into simpler substances which can be used by the body cells, and provide energy and nutrients. This food consists of plants and other animals.

All animals need to breathe. Basically, animals breathe in air and breathe out air with less oxygen and more carbon dioxide. The oxygen is used to release energy from food and is carried around the body in a transport system such as blood. All animals are capable of growth and reproduction.

Plants have many life processes such as nutrition, growth and reproduction which are common to all species. Green plants are the only living things which can produce their own food, by photosynthesis whereby sunlight, carbon dioxide, water and chlorophyll in the leaves are used to make a type of sugar (oxygen is given off from this process).

Flowering plants have specialised parts which help them grow and survive. The roots are used to anchor the plant as well as helping to take in important nutrients and water from the soil. Stems produce and support the leaves, conduct water and nutrients from the soil to the leaves, conduct food made in the leaves to other parts of the plant, and produce and support flowers and fruit. The leaves produce food through photosynthesis and allow the plant to lose water through transpiration. The flowers contain the reproductive organs.

A **habitat** is a place where animals and plants live. It includes the whole surrounding area from which the animal or plant obtains all that it needs to survive. Most animals and plants are specially adapted to live in a particular habitat and have developed special body parts and features to help them do this.

Food chains show the feeding relationships between animals and plants. A plant is eaten by an animal which in turn is eaten by another animal and so on until the carnivore at the top of the food chain is reached. Green plants are producers, animals are consumers and some living things are decomposers. Because green plants are the only producers, they provide food for many other living things, therefore, most food chains begin with a green plant.

Notes on individual activities

Page 5: Animals

Key idea: To promote a discussion about the processes common to all animals, including humans.
Likely outcome: Statements common to all animals are: can eat and drink, can breathe, can grow, can move, can have young. Most animals can hunt for food, but a few animals are sessile.
Extension: Make lists of animals relating to each statement, for example, a list of animals which can lay eggs and discuss the differences between animals.

Page 6: Sorting animals

Key idea: To introduce animal classification.
Likely outcome: Reptiles – crocodile, snake, lizard; Fish – eel, stingray, shark; Birds – owl, duck, ostrich; Amphibians – toad, salamander; Mammals – human, whale, kangaroo, badger.
Extension: Find out the names of 5–10 British animals for each group. Find out more detailed information and create a computer data base.

Page 7: Minibeast movement

Key ideas: The movement of the snail, earthworm and woodlouse and the types of surfaces these creatures can move well on.
Likely outcome: Snails move by wavelike muscular contractions along the bottom of the foot aided by a track of slime; they find it easier to move on smooth surfaces. Earthworms move by muscular movements along their body. They also produce slime which may help them to move in soil. They find it easier to move on smooth surfaces. Woodlice have a flattened body with seven pairs of legs. The body is segmented which aids movement over uneven surfaces.

Page 8: What do minibeasts eat?

Key idea: To investigate the types of food eaten by snails, earwigs, woodlice and beetles.
Likely outcome: Results will vary. These animals usually eat at night so keep the containers in the dark or cover them and partially remove when observing.
Extension: Carry out an investigation of the types of food that birds prefer to eat.

Page 9: Animal growth

Key ideas: The concept of growth in animals. To find out the children's increase in weight since birth.
Likely outcome: Amount of weight gained – mole 93.5g, hedgehog 834g, red fox 5900g, red squirrel 288g, weasel 85g, humans 55,700g (adult weight). To make conversions from pounds and ounces to grams take 1 ounce = 28.350 grams, 1 pound = 0.454 kilogram and 1 stone = 6.350 kilograms.

Some children may not know their birth weight (perhaps because of adoption) and this should be handled sensitively in class. Suggest these children enter the average weight as in the table.
Extension: Birth length could be compared with current height in the same way and another graph completed. Enter the information into a computer database program to create tables and graphs.

Page 10: Animal life-cycles

Key ideas: To compare the life-cycles of different animals. To introduce the concept of metamorphosis.
Likely outcome: Things which are the same – mating takes place before young are born, the female produces eggs, the young grow into adults. Things which are different – the young do not always look like the parents, some animals undergo changes in shape and form before becoming an adult, cats give birth to live young whereas insects lay eggs.
Extension: Observe insect development first-hand. Meal-worm beetles (obtained from pet or fishing shops) are ideal.

Page 11: Identifying some British birds

Key idea: To introduce the concept of using a key to identify animals.
Likely outcome: 1 – mallard, 2 – oyster-catcher, 3 – long-eared owl, 4 – pink-footed goose, 5 – barn owl, 6 – curlew.
Extension: Ask the children to make up another key using the same birds but with different questions.

Page 12: Minibeast sampling

Key idea: To study the difference between animals found in different habitats.

Extension: Discuss the differences/similarities of the creatures found at each site. What features do they have which help them to survive where they live?

Page 13: Animal adaptations

Key idea: To develop an awareness that animals have special adaptations or life-cycle features which are suited to the habitat in which they live.
Likely outcome: Animals which would live near or in a pond are: grass snake, heron, dragonfly, frog, newt tadpole and ramshorn snail.
Extension: Find out about the animals which live in three other habitats, for example woodlands, grasslands and meadows.

Page 14: Pond survey

Key ideas: To carry out field work in the local area. To investigate the types of animals found in different parts of the pond. To use a table to record results.
Likely outcome: Surface dwellers – pond skater, pond snail, water boatman, water beetle; bottom dwellers – dragonfly nymph, freshwater shrimp. Some of these animals will be found in several areas in the pond, especially good swimmers such as beetles.
Extension: Visit the pond at different times of the year to find out how the seasons affect pond life.

Page 15: Food chains

Key ideas: To introduce the terms producer and consumer. To work out possible food chains.
Likely outcome: Grass – P, hedgehog – C, shrub – P, rabbit – C, roe deer – C, wheat – P, flowering plant – P, vole – C, slug – C, tawny owl – C, human – C, fox – C. Possible food chains are: shrub → slug → hedgehog; wheat → vole → tawny owl; grass → roe deer → human; grass → rabbit → human; wheat → vole → fox.
Extension: Find out what other animals eat. Enter this information into a suitable computer program to make tables and graphs about food sources. Use this information to compile more detailed food chains.

Page 16: Plants

Key ideas: Processes which are common to all plants. Names of parts of non-flowering and flowering plants.
Likely outcome: All plants: can grow, need water, can reproduce, can respire, need nutrients. Parts of daisy (from top): petal, stem, leaf, root.

Page 17: Sorting plants

Key ideas: To introduce the idea of plant classification. To sort plants into groups.
Likely outcome: Flowering plants – rose, daisy, bean, oak; Conifers – Douglas fir, Scots pine, juniper, cypress; Mosses and liverworts – sphagnum moss, marchantia; Ferns – bracken fern, tree fern; Fungi – mushroom, toadstool; Algae – sea lettuce, seaweed.
Extension: Make books of each plant group. Include drawings/photographs of local plants.

Page 18: Roots

Key ideas: To observe the roots of a plant and its capillary action. What happens when roots grow?
Likely outcome: A plant has roots to anchor it into the ground and to help in the uptake of water and nutrients. The water from the jar will be soaked up by the cotton cloth and will be transferred to the saucer by capillary action. This is similar to the way a root soaks up water. Roots will grow from the spider plantlet's base.
Extension: Compare the roots from different plants. Find out about tap and fibrous root systems.

Page 19: Stems

Key ideas: To observe the stems of three different flowers. To make observational notes and drawings.
Extension: Study different stems in a garden or wood and observe their similarities and differences.

Page 20: Leaves

Key ideas: Plants lose water through their leaves (transpire). To consider evaporation.
Likely outcome: The experiment is trying to show that plants lose water through their leaves. The oil has been placed in the jars to stop the water from evaporating. The jar with no oil in it should lose more water than all the others because water will escape from the leaves as well as evaporating from the water in the jar. The branch with no leaves should lose the least water.
Extension: Make a graph of the water levels in each jar for each observation day.

Page 21: Flowers

Key ideas: To reinforce the names of flower parts and knowledge of flower structure.
Extension: Challenge the children to make their own models of common flowers (rose, dandelion).

Page 22: The life-cycle of a flowering plant

Key ideas: The life-cycle of flowering plants.
Extension: Find out about the life-cycle of local trees and relate this to seasonal changes.

Page 23: Seed dispersal

Key idea: The four main methods of seed dispersal – wind, animal, explosion and water.
Likely outcome: Possible answers: wind – the dandelion has a parachute effect helping the seed float in the air; animal – the blackberry is small and round and easy to swallow, the burdock has lots of spiny parts which catch in the fur of an animal; explosion – the lupin has a long seed pod and the seeds are well spaced out so that when the pod opens the seeds are spread over a wide area; water – the coconut is completely sealed and waterproof so that water will not get inside and sink it.

The seed examples are dispersed in the following way: broom – explosion; elderberry – animal;

sycamore – wind; agrimony – animal; ash – wind; water lily – water.
Extension: Make large wall posters showing types of dispersal.

Page 24: Bean seedlings
Key ideas: To interpret results obtained from an investigation. To make a comparative investigation about seedling growth.
Likely outcome: Possible answers to questions:
1 Nadeem and Paul were investigating the effects of temperature and amount of light on seed germination and plant growth; **2** The seed in the fridge may germinate but it will not grow due to a low temperature and lack of sunlight; **3** Seeds do not need sunlight to germinate but the young seedlings need it to grow strong because the green pigment chlorophyll is only made in sunlight. The plant in the dark will eventually die; **4** Green plants need sunlight (as well as water, carbon dioxide and chlorophyll) to make their own food.
Extension: Investigate other variables affecting plant growth (type of compost or amount of water).

Page 25: How much light do plants need?
Key idea: To investigate how plant growth is affected by the amount of sunlight it receives.
Likely outcome: The seedlings with the greatest amount of sunlight should grow best. Plants grow towards sunlight (phototropism) so the seedlings will bend towards the light source.
Extension: How do plants which cannot make their own food, such as fungi, get their food?

Page 26: Tree leaves
Key ideas: Close observations of leaf structure and types. To practise sorting skills.
Likely outcome: The leaves could be sorted according to: edge type (wavy, jagged or smooth), shape of veins, simple or compound leaf, shape, and number of leaflets on one stem.
Extension: Ask the children to use reference books to help them draw the leaves of other trees.

Page 27: Plant habitats
Key idea: To compare the plants found in two different local habitats.
Extension: The information gathered could be made into a book which has drawings, photographs and writing about the plants found in the two areas.

Page 28: Plant adaptations
Key ideas: Plant survival in deserts and water. To discuss how plants are adapted to their environment.
Likely outcome: The cactus is adapted to desert life in the following ways: the roots spread a long way and are close to the soil surface to obtain as much water as possible, the stem is large to store water, the plant is shaped so that water runs off it into the roots, the shiny surface of the plant reflects light and the leaves are reduced to spines to reduce water loss so the plant does not overheat.

The water lily is adapted to life in water in the following ways: the leaves are flat so that a large surface area faces the sun, the waxy surface of the leaves prevents them from becoming waterlogged and sinking, it produces seeds which can float, it has air spaces which help it to float, and the long stem has roots which grow into the mud to anchor it.
Extension: Observe the features of a cactus by providing a house plant example. Compare the cactus to plants found in the local area or in gardens.

Page 29: Identifying British wildflowers
Key idea: To use a key to identify wildflowers.
Likely outcome: A – bladder campion, B – common poppy, C – water plantain, D – primrose, E – common centuary, F – marsh marigold.

Page 30: My plant study
Key ideas: A field study of a plant in the local area. To make detailed observational notes and drawings.
Extension: Enter the information gathered into a computer database program, so that the information gathered could be interrogated.

Page 31: Micro-organisms
Key idea: Harmful effects of micro-organisms can be prevented when handling and storing food.
Likely outcome: Washing hands gets rid of many bacteria which could cause food to become contaminated; low temperatures do not destroy bacteria but prevent them from multiplying further; high cooking temperatures destroy bacteria, making the food safe to eat if eaten immediately; the cooking or washing processes involved in canning and bottling remove bacteria and the sealed containers eliminate air which can carry the bacteria.

Bacteria need these conditions to grow: moisture, oxygen, warm temperature, lack of direct sunlight.
Extension: The children could investigate the effects of bacteria on food by placing bread in sealed plastic bags and putting one sample in the fridge and keeping another at room temperature to observe the differences in food deterioration. Remind them not to open the bags or touch the mouldy bread.

Page 32: True or false?
Key ideas: To promote a discussion about the processes common to plants and animals. To provide assessment of the activities covered in this book.
Likely outcome: 1 – T, 2 – F, 3 – T, 4 – T, 5 – F, 6 – F, 7 – T, 8 – T, 9 – T, 10 – T, 11 – F, 12 – F, 13 – T, 14 – F, 15 – T, 16 – T, 17 – F, 18 – F, 19 – F, 20 – F, 21 – T, 22 – F.
Extension: The children could make a book or wall display about plants and animals, showing the characteristics and processes common to them.

▲ Name ______________________________

Animals

You will need: scissors; glue; A4 paper.

▲ What things do **all** animals have in common? Cut out the statements below. Sort them into two groups:

1 things which relate to all animals;
2 things which relate to only some animals.

Do others agree with you? Compare your lists with others.

▲ Cut out the picture of the animals and glue this on to a piece of paper. Glue all the statements in group 1 underneath. Make a heading: **All animals have these things in common**. Add your own drawings of other animals.

can eat and drink	can talk
can live in the water	builds a nest
can breathe	can swim
can fly	can shed its skin
can climb trees	can grow
can move	can have young
lays eggs	can walk
can hunt for food	feeds its young on milk
can sing	has hair
has fur	can change colour
eats other animals	eats plants

▲ Find out all you can about one animal. Make a fact sheet about it.

▲ Name ______________________________

Sorting animals

You will need: a pencil; reference books on animals.

Scientists sort animals into groups to make their identification easier. Vertebrates (animals with a spinal cord and backbone) are sorted into five main groups – fish, amphibians, reptiles, birds and mammals.

Reptiles
- covered in scales
- cold-blooded
- lay eggs with a soft shell

____

____

____

Amphibians
- cold-blooded
- begin life in water but adults can live on land
- moist skin

____

____

Birds
- have feathers
- have wings
- two legs
- lay eggs with a hard shell
- warm-blooded

____

____

____

Fish
- cold-blooded
- live and breathe in water
- have fins
- most have scales
- most have gills

____

____

____

Mammals
- warm-blooded
- feed young on milk
- give birth to live young
- have hair or fur

____

____

____

____

▲ Use the descriptions above to sort these animals into the correct group. Write the name of each animal in the spaces provided.

human owl badger snake eel lizard crocodile whale shark duck toad stingray salamander kangaroo ostrich

▲ Find out how invertebrate animals are sorted.

▲ Name ______________________

Minibeast movement

You will need: snails; worms; woodlice; a pencil; plastic containers to put minibeasts in; materials listed in the 'type of surface' table below.

▲ Do minibeasts move in the same way? What body parts do they use? Can they move on all surfaces? Complete these activities to find out.

	Draw your minibeast here	Describe how it moves. What body parts does it use?
snail		
earthworm		
woodlouse		

▲ Now see if your minibeast can move over different surfaces. Tick the surfaces each creature can move well on.

Type of surface	snail	worm	louse
rough wood			
smooth wood			
sandpaper			
wet sponge			
glass			
plastic			
woollen cloth			
corrugated card			
cotton wool			
aluminium foil			
velvet cloth			

▲ Use another piece of paper to describe how the minibeasts moved on each surface. What problems did they have?

▲ Test some more surfaces. Do minibeasts prefer dry or damp conditions? Why?

▲ Name ______________________________

What do minibeasts eat?

You will need: some snails, woodlice, earwigs and beetles; four glass or plastic aquariums or plastic lunch boxes; some leaves from five different outdoor plants; some fruit such as an apple, grapes and a banana; four different flowers; some bark and twigs; a pencil; four small cardboard boxes; scissors; a knife; a sponge; water; clear food wrap.

▲ What do minibeasts prefer to eat? Carry out this investigation to find out. Set up four aquariums, all exactly the same as the one opposite. Place the aquariums in a dark place with a different minibeast in each one.

Can you predict which foods they might eat?

▲ Make daily observations of each aquarium. Write down if the minibeasts have visited or eaten any of the foods in the table below.

What have you found out?

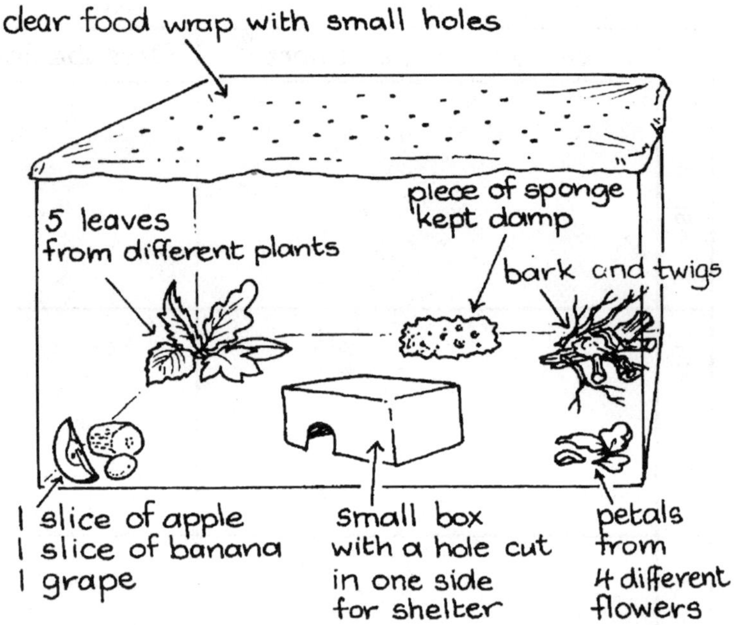

▲ Return the minibeasts to where you found them when you have finished your investigation.

Minibeast	Day	Leaves	Flowers	Fruit	Bark
 snail	Day 1				
	Day 2				
	Day 3				
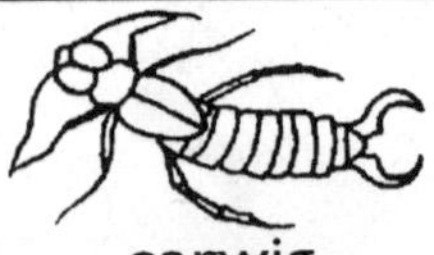 earwig	Day 1				
	Day 2				
	Day 3				
 woodlouse	Day 1				
	Day 2				
	Day 3				
 beetle	Day 1				
	Day 2				
	Day 3				

▲ Repeat the experiment using different foods or use the same foods with different minibeasts. Compare the results.

▲ Name ____________________________

Animal growth

You will need: a pencil; bathroom scales.

All animals grow. Some animals take longer to grow than others. Some animals grow larger than others. Most animals grow much larger as they get older. Their growth usually stops when they are adults.

▲ Look at the table below. It compares the birth weight and adult weight of some common animals, including us!

Animal	Average weight at birth	Average adult weight	Amount of weight gained from birth to adulthood
mole	3.5 g	97 g	
hedgehog	16 g	850 g	
red fox	100 g	6000 g	
red squirrel	12 g	300 g	
weasel	2 g	87 g	
human	3300g	59,000g	

▲ Work out how much weight each animal gains from birth to adulthood. Write your answers in the table.

▲ Complete the table below to find out how much you and some of your friends have grown since birth.

Name	Birth weight	Current weight	Weight gained

▲ Make a graph of these weights.

▲ Name ________________________

Animal life-cycles

You will need: a pencil; frog spawn; an ice-cream container or glass jar; reference books on frogs.

Many animals begin life as eggs inside their mother. When they are born, they are miniature versions of their parents. As they get older they grow in size but do not change the basic shape they were born with. Some animals, however, completely change their shape and form as they grow.

▲ Look at the two life-cycles below to compare how each animal develops.

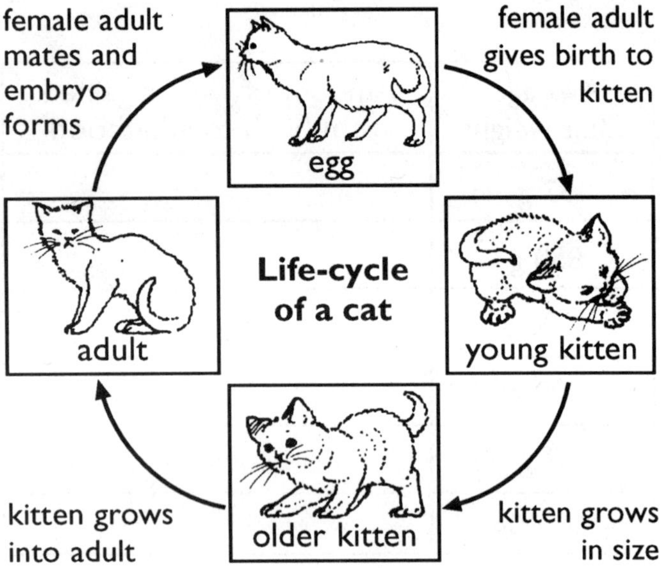

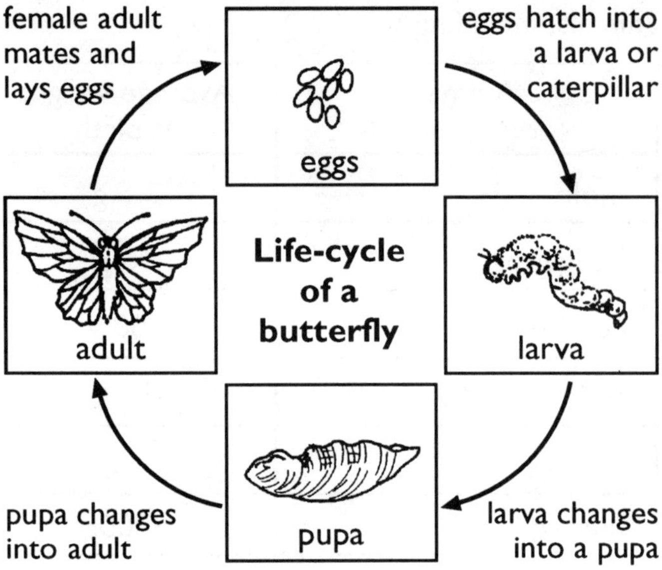

What is the same about both life-cycles? ________________________

____

What is different about both life-cycles? ________________________

____

When animals totally change shape and form during the life-cycle, the process is called metamorphosis. The life-cycle of the frog changes in this way.

▲ Obtain a few frog eggs and place them in a container with pond water. Keep a diary of the changes which take place. Complete the life-cycle chart opposite. Use reference books if frog spawn is not available.

▲ Find out about the life-cycles of other animals.

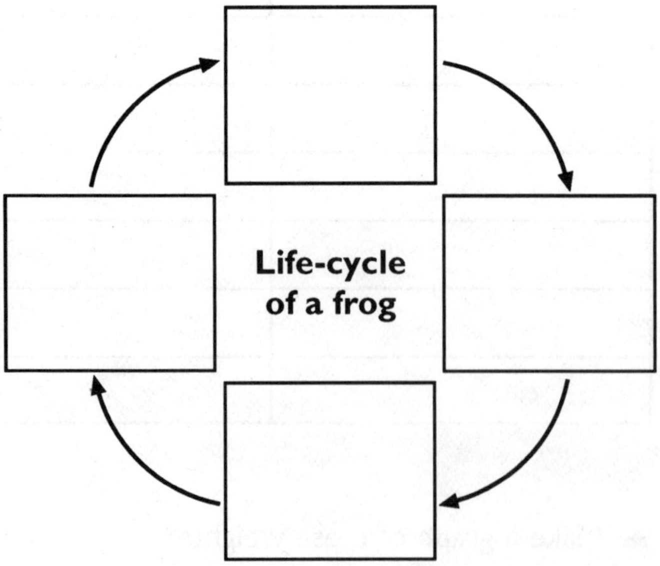

▲ Name ______________________________

Identifying some British birds

You will need: a pencil.

Keys are often used in science to find out the name of a living thing. Many keys involve working through a set of questions until you find the name which best fits the thing you are trying to identify.

▲ Use the key below to help you name these British birds. Write the name of each bird next to its picture. Compare your answers with others. Do they agree?

1 ____________________

2 ____________________

3 ____________________

4 ____________________

5 ____________________

6 ____________________

Do the eyes face the front?

- Yes — Does it have long 'ear' tufts?
  - Yes — Long-eared owl
  - No — Barn owl
- No — Does it have webbed feet?
  - Yes — Does it have a long neck?
    - Yes — Pink-footed goose
    - No — Mallard
  - No — Does it have a long, downturned bill?
    - Yes — Curlew
    - No — Oyster-catcher

▲ Make up your own key to identify some other birds or animals.

▲ Name ______________________________

Minibeast sampling

You will need: a hoop; a hand lens; a dip net; a pencil; reference books on minibeasts to help with identification.

▲ Compare the minibeasts found in three different areas:

A a rocky place;
B a grassy place;
C a pond.

Put your hoop down in each area – it will float on the pond. Look for minibeasts in the space inside your hoop. Count the number of different creatures. Use books to try and name them. Use a dip net in the pond to sweep through the water. What creatures do you catch?

▲ Complete the table below for each area.

Area	Number found	Names of minibeasts found	Drawing of one minibeast
 rocky place			
 grassy place			
 pond			

▲ Find out more information about one minibeast in each area. What special features do they have which help them to live in each place?

▲ Name ______________________________

Animal adaptations

You will need: scissors; a pencil; compasses; colouring pencils; glue; A4 paper; a large piece of paper or card.

▲ Draw two circles (radius 5cm) on A4 paper. Draw a pond scene inside one circle and a woodland inside the other. Colour, label and cut them out. Cut out each animal card below. Would the animal live in or near a pond or a wood? Why? Do others agree? Glue the circles and matching animal cards on to a large piece of paper to make a poster of animal adaptations.

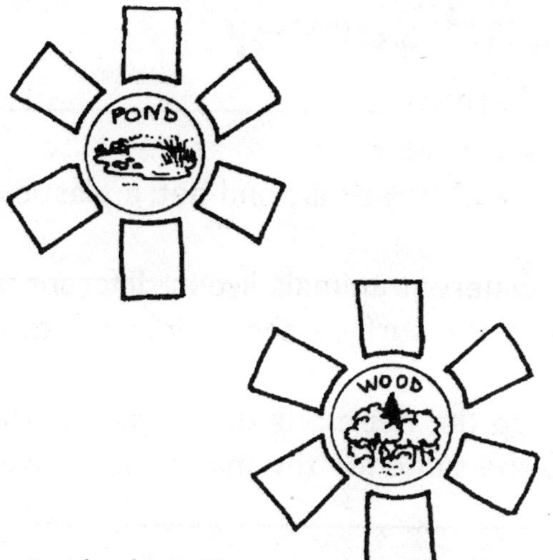

Animal adaptations

Slow worm

Eats slugs, worms and spiders. Prefers dry areas.

Ramshorn snail

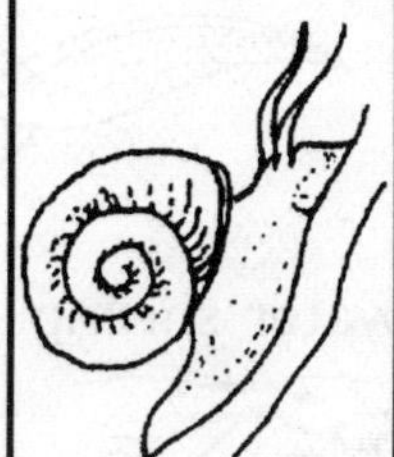

Eats algae. Lays eggs in jelly.

Grey heron

Eats fish.

Mottled umber moth

Caterpillars eat deciduous leaves.

Dragonfly

Lays eggs on water plants. Nymphs live in water.

Badger

Digs underground set. Eats worms, small mammals, roots, fruit and seeds.

Jay

Eats nuts and eggs. Builds nest in small trees.

Grass snake

Eats frogs, fish and small rodents.

Robber-fly

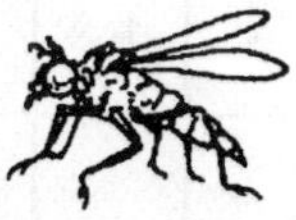

Lives among plants. Larvae live in soil.

Newt tadpole

Breathes with gills.

Lizard

Eats insects. Likes to bask in sun. Likes old walls.

Frog

Lays its eggs in water. Young develop in water.

▲ Visit a pond and a woodland. Draw some of the animals you find. Write down how you think they are suited to their habitat.

Pond survey

▲ Name ______________________ Date ______________________

You will need: a pond net; a plastic container; a pencil; paper; a clipboard.

▲ Different animals live in different parts of a pond. Do this survey to find out which animals live at the surface, the middle and the bottom of a pond.

Sweep the net along the surface of the pond several times. Record what you find in the table. Do the same for the middle and lower depths of the pond.

a water boatman

b dragonfly nymph

c pond skater

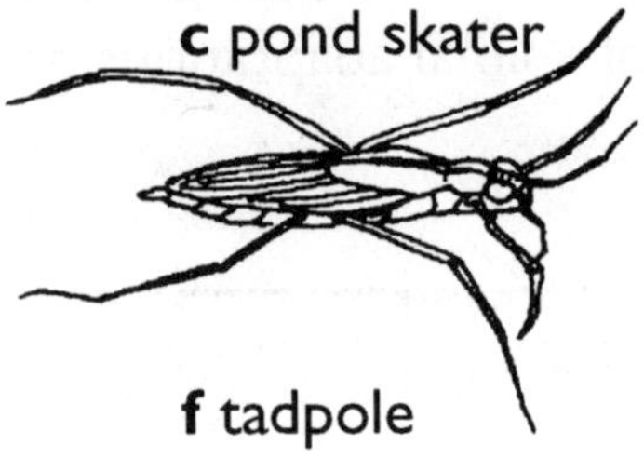

d water flea

e water beetle

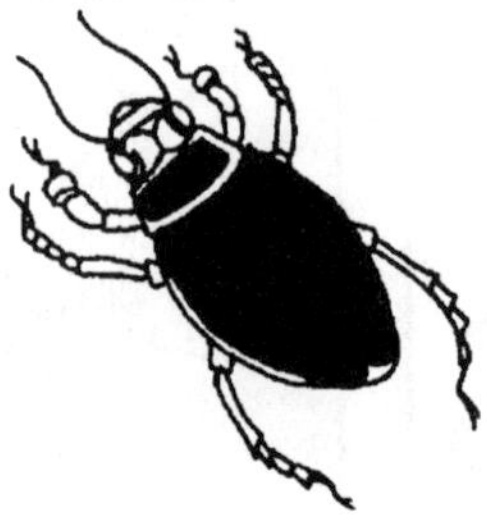

f tadpole

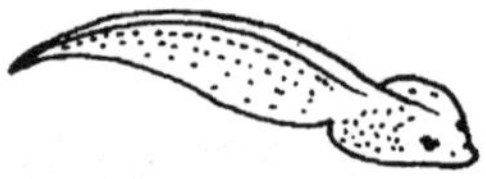

g pond snail

h freshwater shrimp

▲ Tick the animals you find in each area.

Pond area	**Animal**								**Other animals (write name)**	
	a	b	c	d	e	f	g	h		
surface										
middle										
bottom										

▲ Draw a picture of an animal from each area of the pond on some paper.

▲ Compare what you found with others.

▲ Find out more about some of these animals.

▲ Name ______________________________

Food chains

You will need: a pencil.

Living things can be either producers or consumers. Green plants are *producers*. They are able to manufacture their own food using a process called photosynthesis. *Consumers* are living things which eat other living things.

▲ Look at the plants and animals below. Decide if each is a producer (P) or consumer (C). Write the letter P or C in the box for each one.

grass ☐	hedgehog ☐	shrub ☐	rabbit ☐	roe deer ☐	wheat ☐
	 eats slugs, worms and insects		 eats grass	 eats grass	
flowering plant ☐	vole ☐	slug ☐	tawny owl ☐	human ☐	fox ☐
	 eats grass and wheat	 eats leaves	 eats mice and voles	 eats plants and animals	 eats rabbits, mice and voles

Food chains show the feeding relationships between living things. Nearly all food chains begin with a green plant or producer. The plant is eaten by an animal, which in turn is eaten by another animal and so on.

▲ Use the plants and animals above to write down some food chains. Here is one example for you:

grass ⟶ rabbit ⟶ fox

▲ Find out what other animals eat and make some more food chains.

▲ Name ______________________

Plants

You will need: a pencil.

▲ What things do all plants have in common? Look at the statements below. Tick those which you think are true of all plants. Compare your answers with others. Do they agree?

have roots		can reproduce	
can grow		have seeds	
have leaves		need sunlight to grow	
need water to grow		can respire (breathe)	
cannot move		need nutrients to grow	
make their own food		have stems	

▲ Plants have different parts too. Look at the two plants below. What is different about them? Label the parts of the flowering plant.

mushroom

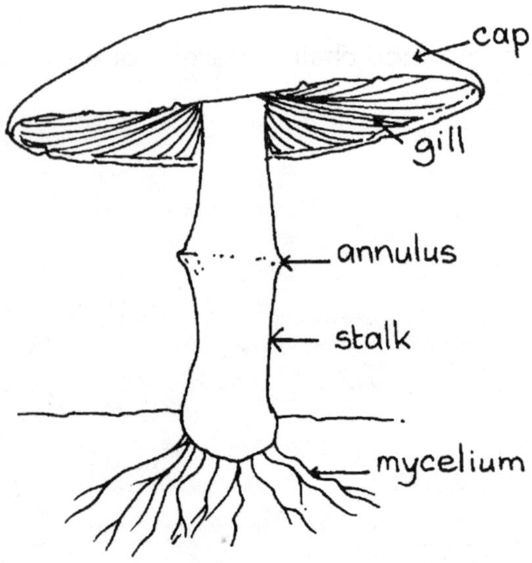

daisy

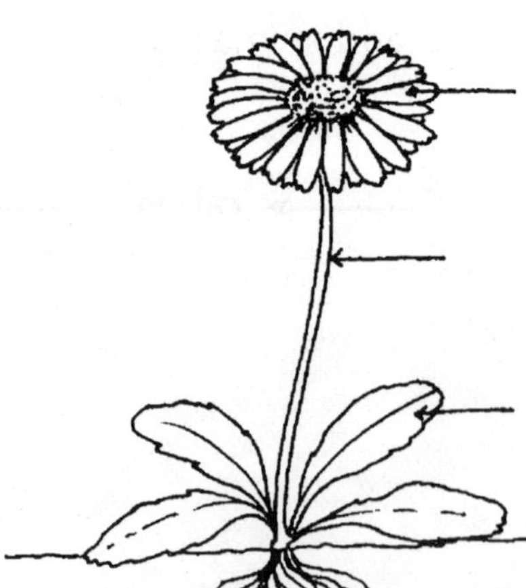

▲ Find out all you can about one plant. Make a fact sheet about it.

▲ Name ______________________

Sorting plants

You will need: a pencil.

Scientists sort plants into groups to make their identification easier. Here is a simple classification of plants.

Flowering plants
- stems, roots, leaves, flowers
- can make own food
- reproduce by seeds

____

____

____

____

Conifers
- stems, roots, leaves, no true flowers
- can make own food
- reproduce by seeds; seeds usually in cones

____

____

____

____

Fungi
- no roots, stems, leaves or flowers
- cannot make own food; live on dead matter
- reproduce by spores

____

____

Algae
- no stems, roots or leaves
- can make own food
- usually live in water

____

____

Mosses and liverworts
- no true stems, roots, leaves or flowers
- can make own food
- reproduce by spores
- usually small

____

____

Ferns
- stems, roots, leaves, but no flowers
- can make own food
- reproduce by spores

____

____

▲ Use the descriptions above to sort these plants into the correct group. Write the name of each plant in the spaces provided.

cypress mushroom oak marchantia rose daisy

toadstool

tree fern Douglas fir

bean sphagnum moss

seaweed

sea lettuce Scots pine juniper bracken fern

▲ Use reference books to help you name examples of each plant group found in your local area.

▲ Name ______________________

Roots

You will need: a small pot plant (such as a spider plant); a jar; water; a plantlet from the spider plant; a saucer; a small piece of cotton cloth; a newspaper; a pencil.

▲ Carefully remove the pot plant from its container. Gently remove the soil from the roots (use newspaper to collect the soil). Look closely at the roots.

What colour are they? ______________________

Describe what they look like. ______________________

____

Can you suggest why a plant has roots? ______________________

____

▲ How do roots soak up water? Do this simple experiment to show capillary action:

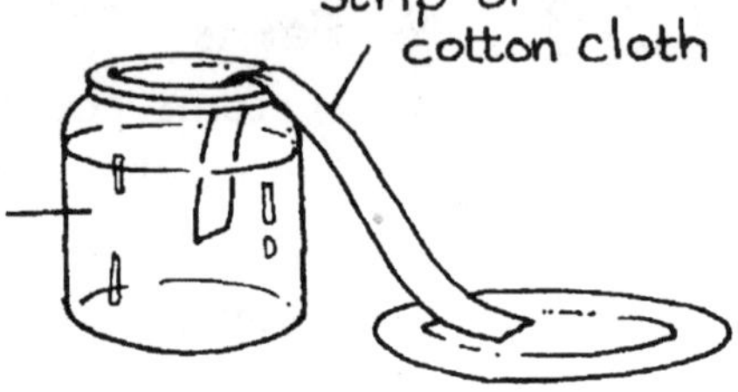

What do you think will happen?

____

Leave for several hours. Observe what happens. Discuss what is happening.

▲ Now observe some roots growing. Place a plantlet from a spider plant in a jar of water. Observe what happens over the next few weeks. Record the results here:

Day	Description – what happens?
5	
10	
15	
20	
25	
30	
35	

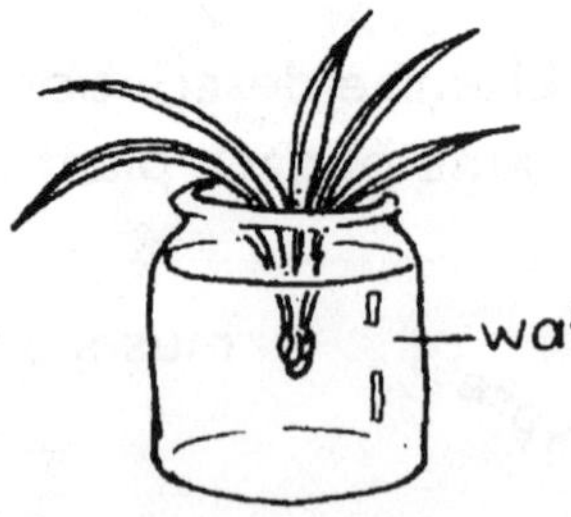

▲ Grow roots in other ways, for example:

1 cuttings in water

2 growing seeds.

Compare the roots which grow.

▲ Name ______________________________

Stems

You will need: a pencil; thin string (about 10cm in length); a ruler; colouring pencils; three cut flowers with different stems (such as a rose, a lily and a poppy).

The stems of plants vary a great deal. Some stems grow underground (such as in the potato), some run along the ground (such as strawberries), but most stems grow tall and upright.

▲ Look closely at the stems of three flowers. Write down what you think the stems are used for in a plant.

____

____

▲ Now complete a detailed study of the stems, by filling in each section below. Use the string to measure the stem circumference.

Plant details	**Drawing of stem**	**Description of stem** (colour, texture, firmness, shape, features)
Plant name ____________ Circumference of stem – thickest part ________ – thinnest part ________ Number of leaves on stem ____ Number of flowers on stem ____		
Plant name ____________ Circumference of stem – thickest part ________ – thinnest part ________ Number of leaves on stem ____ Number of flowers on stem ____		
Plant name ____________ Circumference of stem – thickest part ________ – thinnest part ________ Number of leaves on stem ____ Number of flowers on stem ____		

▲ Make a study of the stems on woody plants such as trees. Compare these stems with those of the flowers.

▲ Name ______________________________

Leaves

You will need: four jars (all the same size); four small tree branches (such as ash); water; a measuring jug; cooking oil; masking tape; a ruler; a pencil; scissors.

▲ What happens to the water taken up by plants? Do this experiment to find out. Set up four jars like this:

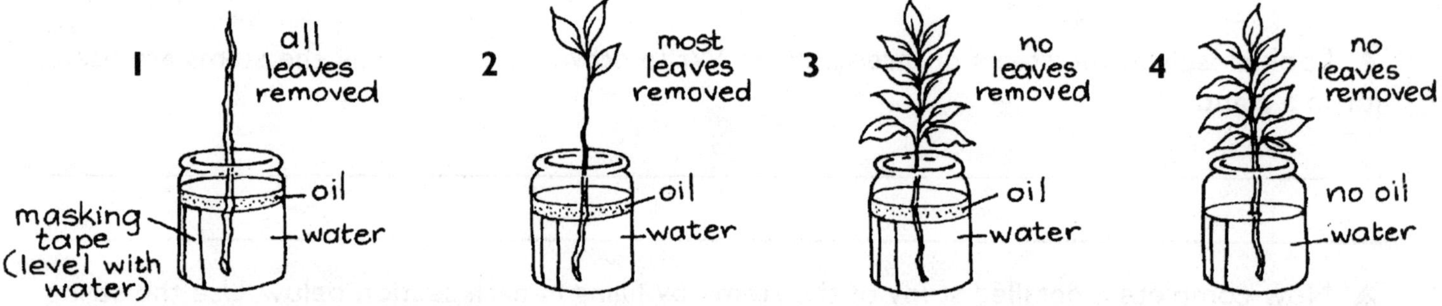

Cut the branches so they are all the same size. Pour the same measured amount of water into each jar (¾ full). Put a thick covering of oil in three of the jars. Mark off the water levels on the masking tape.

Place all the jars in sunlight. Measure the water level from the top of the water to the base of the jar. Record in the table below. Observe and record the water level every three days.

What do you think the experiment is trying to find out? ______________________________

____

How have you made the test fair? ______________________________

____

Can you suggest why you have put oil into three of the jars? ______________________________

____

Condition	Prediction – what you think will happen	Water level measurements					
		Day 1	Day 4	Day 7	Day 10	Day 13	Day 16
1 No leaves Oil							
2 Few leaves Oil							
3 Many leaves Oil							
4 Many leaves No oil							

▲ What do the results show you? Share your ideas with others.

▲ Find out what plants use water for. How does it help them?

▲ Name ______________________________

Flowers

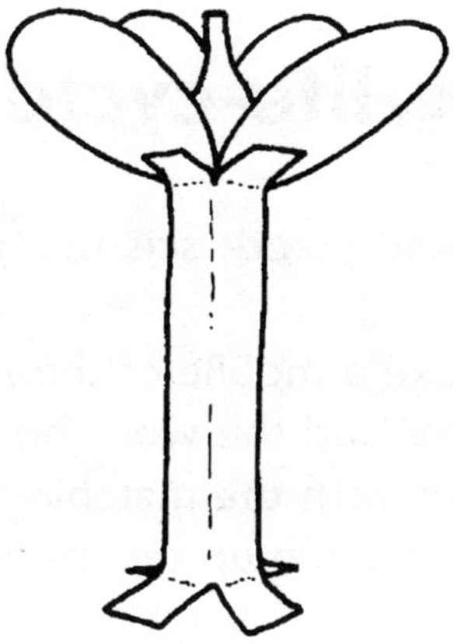

You will need: scissors; glue; a pencil; colouring pencils.

▲ To make this model flower, follow these directions.

1 Write these names in the correct places on the flower parts: stem, petal, pistil, stamen.
2 Colour the flower parts.
3 Cut out the parts.

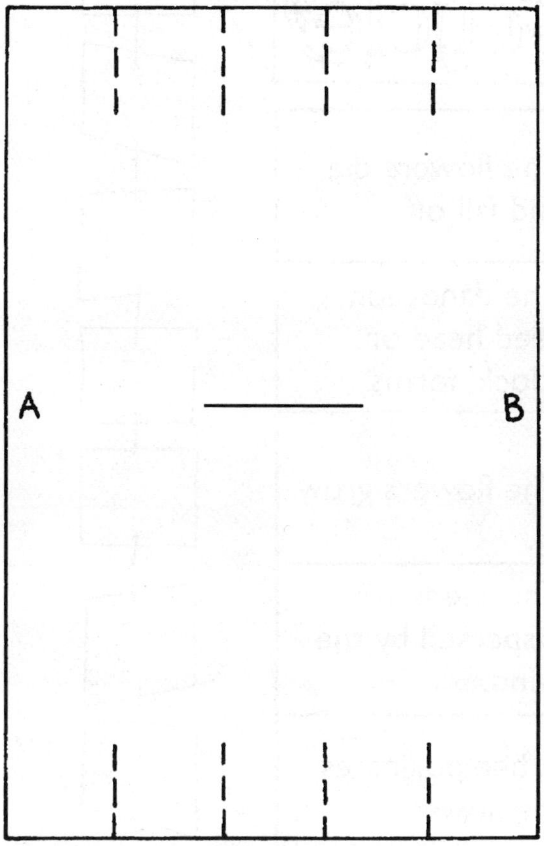

4 Cut along the dotted lines on the stem.
5 Fold the stem into a tube with the label on the outside and glue 'A' to 'B'.
6 Open out the tabs on the top of the tube.

7 Glue the petals to the tabs at the top of the stem.

8 Bend the tab on the base of the pistil and glue this to the centre of the petals.

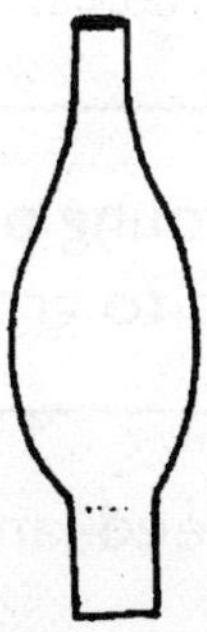

9 Open out the tabs on the bottom of the stem to make the model stand up.

▲ Find out what each of the plant parts do for the flower.

▲ Name ______________________________

The life-cycle of a flowering plant

You will need: scissors; glue; card; cotton thread; colouring pencils.

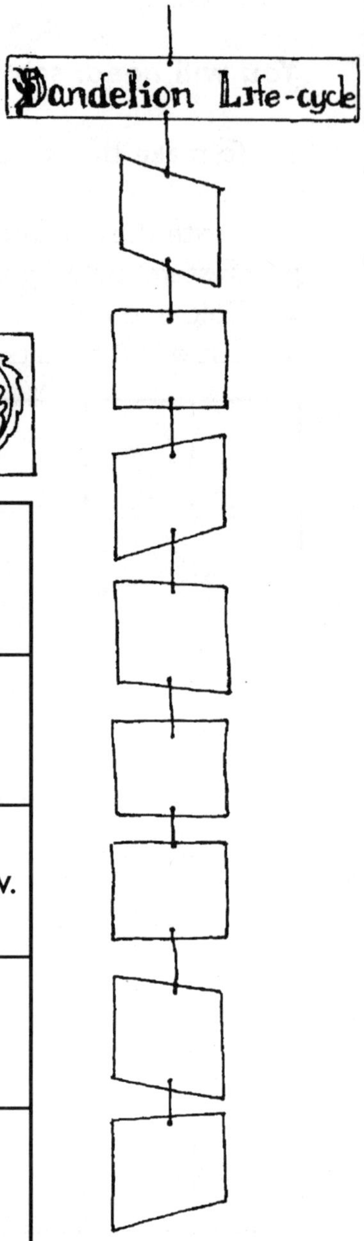

▲ Make a mobile of the life-cycle of the dandelion. First colour the pictures and the word boxes. Cut along the lines. Glue each picture on to card with the matching sentence on the back. Cut out. Use cotton thread to join up the mobile in the correct order.

Dandelion Life-cycle

		The flowers die and fall off. The dandelion seed head or 'clock' forms.
		The flowers grow. The seeds are dispersed by the wind.
		A bee pollinates the flower. The seed germinates.
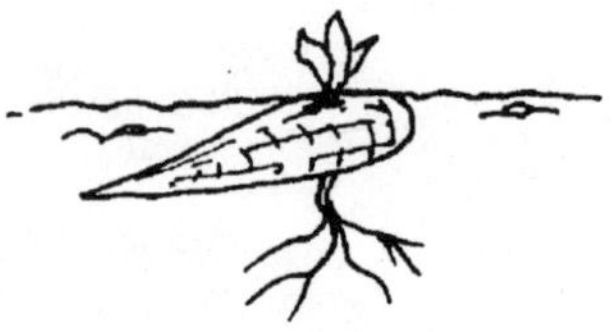		The young plant begins to grow. The seed lands in soil.

▲ Find out about the life-cycle of another plant. Make a mobile of its life-cycle.

▲ Name ______________________________

Seed dispersal

You will need: a pencil.

Many seeds are made in a special way to help them travel a long way when they are dispersed. This allows plants of the same type to grow in new areas and not become too crowded in one place.

▲ Seeds can be dispersed in many different ways. Below are some examples. Look at the shapes of the seeds. Write down your ideas about how the design of the seed might help it to be dispersed in the way it is.

Type of dispersal	Seed example		How I think the seed design helps it to be dispersed
Wind The wind blows the seed away from the parent plant.	 dandelion		
Animal **a** Birds eat the fruit and the seeds pass out in their droppings. **b** The seeds catch in the fur of animals.	**a**  blackberry	**b**  burdock	
Explosion The seeds have an outer pod which splits and pushes the seeds out.	 lupin		
Water The seed floats away in the water of ponds, rivers or oceans.	 coconut		

▲ Now look at these seeds. Decide how they might be dispersed – wind, animal, explosion or water. Write your answer underneath each picture. Do others agree with your choices?

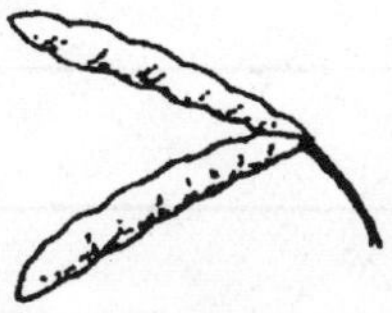 broom	 elderberry	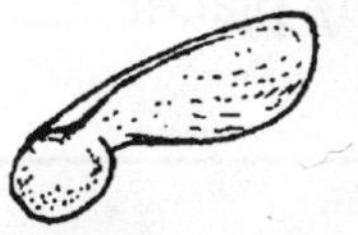 sycamore	 agrimony	 ash	 water lily

▲ Make some model seeds that could be dispersed by the wind. Test them to see which one works best. Why?

▲ Name ______________________________

Bean seedlings

You will need: broad beans; potting compost; three yoghurt pots; water; pencil; paper.

Nadeem and Paul carried out an experiment on growing bean seeds. They got three yoghurt pots and filled them with potting compost. They placed a bean seed inside each pot. They watered the compost when it was dry. They placed one pot in the fridge, one in a cool, dark place and one in a warm, sunny place.

This is what the bean seedlings looked like after four weeks:

1 What do you think Nadeem and Paul were trying to find out? ______________________________

____

2 Why do you think the plant did not grow in the fridge? ______________________________

____

3 Explain why the plant in the cool, dark place grew spindly and yellow.

____

4 Why did the plant grow best in a warm, sunny place? ______________________________

____

▲ Now try out this experiment yourself. Keep a diary of what happens. How do your results compare with Nadeem and Paul's investigation?

▲ Try the same experiment with different seed types. How do the results compare?

▲ Name ______________________________

How much light do plants need?

You will need: bird seed; cotton wool; six saucers; five shoe boxes; scissors; a pencil; water.

▲ Carry out this investigation to find out how much light plants need to grow.

Place some cotton wool in each saucer and add water so that the wool is quite wet. Sprinkle bird seed on to this. Put all the saucers on a table in the sunlight. Keep one saucer uncovered but cover the other saucers with a shoe box in the following way:

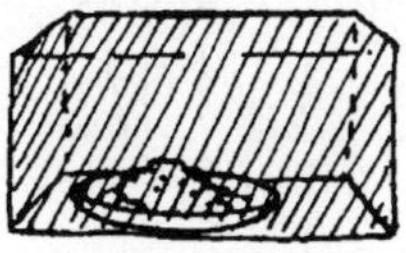

no holes

one small hole

both ends cut out

holes cut out in bottom of all sides

turned upside down

▲ Observe the growth of the seeds over the next few weeks. Keep the cotton wool damp. Record what happens in the table below. Discuss the results. What do they tell you?

Amount of light	What I think will happen (prediction)	What happened (result) Describe what the seedlings looked like
no cover		
no holes		
one small hole		
both ends cut out		
bottom of sides cut out		
box upside down		

▲ Find out how plants use light to help them grow. What function does the leaf have?

▲ Name ______________________________

Tree leaves

You will need: scissors; reference books on trees; paper; glue; pencil.

▲ Cut out the pictures of leaves below. Sort them into groups in some way. Record how you sorted them. Now sort them in a different way. Record this also. How many different ways can you sort the leaves? Share your results with others.

horse chestnut

lime

hazel

beech

oak

ash

walnut

Douglas fir

sycamore

▲ Glue the pictures on to another piece of paper. Use reference books to help you write some information about each type of tree on your sheet of paper. Use this sheet to identify trees in your area.

▲ Name ______________________

Plant habitats

You will need: a pencil; clipboard; plant reference books.

▲ Visit a meadow and complete the chart about the plants which grow there.

▲ Next visit a wood and complete another chart about the plants you find there. Compare your findings with others.

Habitat: ______________	
Tick the plants which grow in this area: trees ☐ grass ☐ mosses ☐ shrubs ☐ fungi ☐ liverworts ☐ flowers ☐ ferns ☐	
What is the main kind of plant? ______________ What is the name of this plant? ______________ Draw two plants you find here:	
What is the tallest plant in this area? ______________ Estimate its height. __________ What is the shortest plant in this area? ______________ Estimate its height. __________ Describe one of the plants you find.	

▲ Visit two other sites such as scrubland, a pond, moor or wasteland. Compare the plants found in each site.

▲ Name ______________________________

Plant adaptations

You will need: a pencil.

Plants have special features which help them to survive in a particular habitat.

▲ Look at the two plants described below. Decide which features you think would help the plant to grow well in its habitat. Write these features underneath each picture. Share your ideas with others. Do they agree?

Cactus – a plant which lives in the desert.	Water lily – a plant which grows in water.
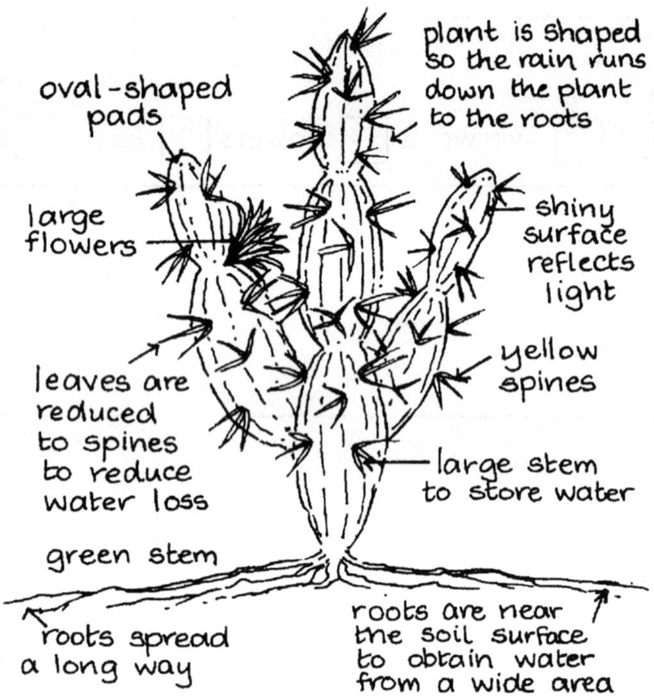	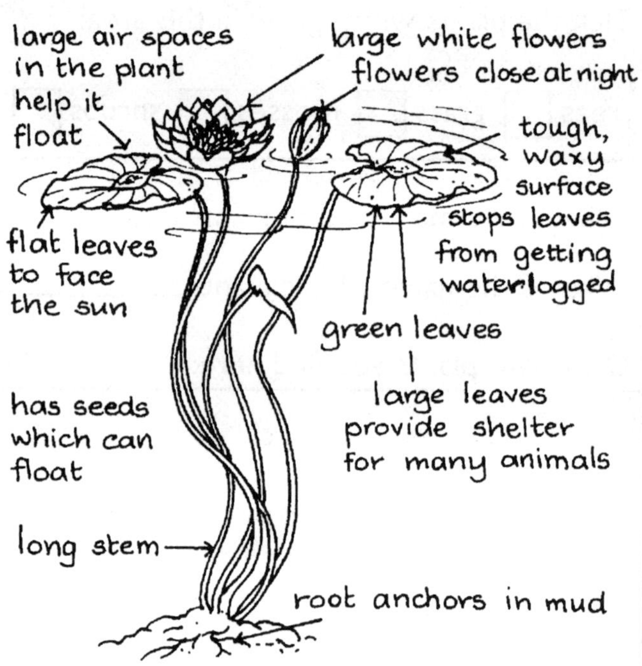
In what ways is the cactus adapted to live in the desert?	In what ways is the water lily adapted to live in water?

▲ Find out how some plants are adapted to living on very cold mountains or in very humid places like rainforests.

▲ Name ______________________________

Identifying British wildflowers

You will need: a pencil.

Keys are used to help identify living things. Many keys involve working through a set of questions until you find the name which best fits the thing you are trying to identify.

Keys encourage us to look very closely at what we want to identify.

▲ Look closely at the drawings of these wildflowers. Use the key to help you name them. Compare your answers with others. Do they agree?

A	B	C	D	E	F
				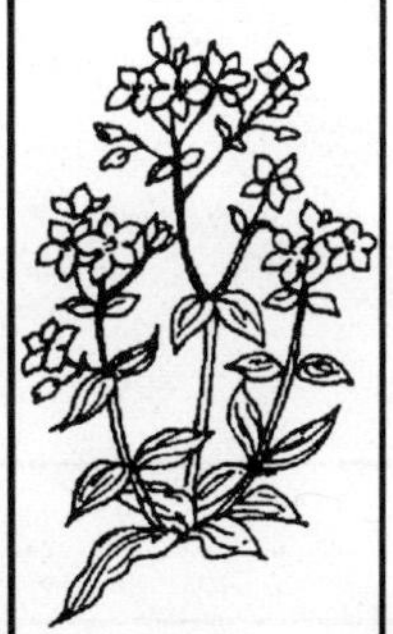	

Write name here

1 Does it have a very long stem?
Yes – go to question 3.
No – go to question 2.

2 Are the leaves large and tapering?
Yes – it's a primrose.
No – it's a marsh-marigold.

3 Is the stem hairy?
Yes – it's a common poppy.
No – go to question 4.

4 Are all the leaves at the base?
Yes – it's a water plantain.
No – go to question 5.

5 Do the leaves have prominent veins?
Yes – it's a common centaury.
No – it's a bladder campion.

▲ Take some photographs of wildflowers in your local area. Find out their names. Make up a key so that others can identify them.

▲ Name ______________________ Date ______________________

My plant study

You will need: a pencil; sticky tape; a plant identification book; a measuring tape.

▲ Use this page to make a detailed study of a plant you have found in your local area.

Where I found it: ______________________

Draw the plant here.	Attach a leaf from the plant here.

Height of plant: ____________ Colour of stem: ____________

Describe the stem/trunk. ______________________

Does it have flowers? If yes, describe them. ______________________

____

Is it growing alone or with other plants of the same type?

____

Can you see any roots? ____________

Describe the soil in which the plant is growing. ______________________

____

How are the leaves arranged on the stem? ______________________

____

Name your plant. ______________________

▲ Make a study of a plant in two different areas such as a field or meadow and a wood. Compare the plants found.

▲ Name ______________________________

Micro-organisms

You will need: a pencil.

Bacteria are microscopic living things. Some bacteria are decomposers which help to get rid of wastes. Other bacteria can cause diseases. We need to look after the food we eat to prevent bacteria making us ill.

▲ Look at each example below. Write down how you think each activity helps to kill bacteria. Share your ideas with others. Do they agree?

1 Washing hands before handling food. 	**2** Putting food in a refrigerator. 
3 Cooking food. 	**4** Bottling and canning food. 

▲ Make a poster telling others how to look after and store food correctly.

▲ Name ____________________

True or false?

You will need: a pencil.

▲ How much do you know about animals and plants? Complete this sheet to find out! Discuss your answers with others. Do they agree?

▲ Put a tick in the appropriate column.

	T	F		T	F
1 All animals eat, drink and move.			12 All plants produce seeds.		
2 Fish are the only animals which breathe in water.			13 Green plants need carbon dioxide, water, sunlight and chlorophyll to make food.		
3 Most mammals give birth to live young.			14 Trees are not plants.		
4 Animals can grow and reproduce.			15 Many flowers are brightly coloured to attract insects to them.		
5 Humans are not animals.			16 Seeds form after pollination takes place.		
6 The young of all animals look like their parents.			17 Seeds are not spread by animals.		
7 Most animals begin life as an egg.			18 Plants can survive without water.		
8 A habitat is the place where plants and animals live.			19 Animals and plants can live anywhere.		
9 Green plants are the only living things that can make their own food.			20 All micro-organisms cause diseases.		
10 A hedgehog is a consumer.			21 Most seeds will germinate in the dark.		
11 Food chains show how living things reproduce.			22 Humans are producers.		

▲ Make your own list of true or false statements about living things. Share it with a friend. Do you agree on the answers?